YouAreNever *Alone*

(Essence of life ....in an authentic way)

Ananya

First Published in April 2022

ISBN: 978-93-5611-439-5

BLUEROSE PUBLISHERS
www.bluerosepublishers.com
info@bluerosepublishers.com
+91 8882 898 898

Cover Design:
Ananya

Typographic Design:
Pooja Sharma

Distributed by: BlueRose, Amazon, Flipkart

"Whenever it hurts deep within, be in the present more.
Healing will come naturally from the....*SOURCE* "

Acknowledgement

At the very onset, I wish to share this with my readers, that ....

I could step into this journey and make it a reality for me today, all because of 'The Divine Blessing's and a constant push from my spiritual guides .

This project is no longer a dream, as my words are in print now and hence, I pay my homage and utmost gratitude to my entire team of spiritual beings.

I take the privilege to thank my son, for being a constant support and motivation to me, since his childhood. I had always wished to fulfill his desire to see me independent and strong. I am glad that I could do so, now.

I sincerely thank a long lost friend who has been an inspiration always, a friend I lost to darkness. The very essence of this creative piece, the content, is an idea that sparked out one evening, over a cup of coffee. I owe my gratitude to this 'Friendly Venture'.

I am immensely grateful, to my Mothers, One.... to whom I shall remain thankful always for giving me this Life. And, am also grateful to mother Earth **Gaia**, for holding me, deep within her crystalline core, in a manner I exist today. Thank you Divine Mother for grounding me, this strong .

Above all, I convey my gratefulness to the most important and wonderful people in my life who have nurtured my childhood, my adolescents, with so much care, and helped me grow up to values I treasure most . They are the most loveable people and I am fortunate to have them in my life and I hold them close to my heart . I am what I am today, for their true and unconditional Love.

Thank you ! Thank you! Thank you !

This book is based on true incidents, and I request my readers, please do not to take it as another contentful reading and leave it aside to stack up your collection of good books, or not so good ones. Through these pages I intend to share certain experiences of some people I know and what they have gone through, as I feel, that these experiences might be of help to many others to understand and take it as guidance, if one can relate to it. Yet, I choose to bottle up the true identities of the characters mentioned here. This is to bestow my respect towards the privacy of the generous souls.

I want my readers to understand, the purpose of my writing this book, and thus join 'Your Hands' with me, in your own unique ways, to bring a change in the society. My intention is, not only to share some people's true and painful experiences of life, just for the sake of sharing, or, simply earning appraisal for myself. I literally want your extended helping hands towards the not so - not always privileged lot amongst us.

Please do help me spread awareness, and bring forth empathic support and care, for our much needy and deserving brethren, all over the World .

One

Its a bright Sunny day today, and I'm loving it, as this is happening after a week's ... long bleak weather. I woke up a happy soul this morning, feeling fresh and lively, after going through a difficult time for months together. Winter is always difficult for me, being a neuropathic patient. It is tough to tackle the climate. But now, spring has entered and so a happy environment is all around me. Fresh and gentle breeze are flowing all over in the atmosphere, birds are chirping delightfully and even the Sky is radiant blue. The day looked promising. I picked up my cup of tea and walked into the garden area under the sunlight, to spend some happy moment with my plants.

Wonderfully enough, the flowers started blooming. Fresh rose buds, some fully bloomed ones, fresh leaves all over looked enchanting. Few days back, the Lilies that were almost fading away, were now growing back. I felt excited, and the happy me, took to watering the plants. I put on some soft music and was enjoying my chores. Suddenly, my mobile started ringing and I looked at the number that flashed on the screen. It was an unknown number and so I avoided it. After a few seconds, there came a second call from the same number. At first, I was hesitant to take the call as I usually avoid unknown numbers. Mostly, calls from unknown numbers would be by mistake, or it would be some promotional ones.

Also, I don't socialize much, so there's a faint chance that it would be someone I know. The phone kept ringing and I felt .... What if someone is trying to reach out to me in urgency, and so I picked the call. The voice sounded quite familiar, yet I couldn't catch who this person was. It was a female voice asking me, "Is this Anna "?

I gently replied "Yes ! But I'm sorry to say that I am failing to identify you from your voice. May I know who's speaking ? "

"Hey, I'm Avantika", she said, "Hope you haven't forgotten me by now "

Oh ! So its Avantika, how can I forget her? We had such wonderful time together during our husband's posting at a remote township. Both of our husbands are in the same organization. Although she was much junior, we jelled together a lot.

"Oh No! Avantika, there's no chance to ever forget you," I said, "but as its been quite a long time now, that we communicated, its lack of my memory power, my dear, and you should keep in mind that I am ageing ".

We both giggled on that note. After a pause, I asked, "So how's life? And where have you been all this time ? "

"I am here, in your city for a short tour" she answered "Can we catch up for old times sake ? "

"Oh ! Why not," I replied, "do come over please, visit my home anytime and whenever you are free from your work ".

"No please, not your home dear, I really want to have a long chat with you. So Madam, I seek your full attention, which otherwise will get diverted into hospitality. I know you so well", prompt came her response.

She sounded tensed, although she tried to express excitement. "Please do take out some time for me, from your busy schedule ", she added.

"Oh ! Come-on !!, I said, "I am super excited to be with you anytime, my dear. So, when do you wish to meet up ? "

"Anytime this afternoon ", she informed, "let's have lunch together "

We fixed 1:30 pm as our scheduled time. She collected my address and said she would pick me up.

Suddenly, it turned out to be a very busy day for me now. I had to finish up my chores and be ready on time. Although there was excitement in the air, I was also continuously wondering, what could be the reason for her decision to meet me outdoor, when she always enjoyed food at my place. 'Anyways, people do change with time ', is what I thought, and got back to finish my work. By 12:30 pm, I was done with all my duties. And now was the actual preparation time. Well ! getting ready to walk out of the house to meet up with friends, is a jolly heck of time for us ladies. I kept pondering on what to wear. After a long time, I was actually feeling excited to dress up.

Normally, these days, I hardly visit anyone. Its only the 'run errands 'outing for me, most of the time. So I hardly bother about what I wear and how I dress, even though this is one form of art that is close to my heart.

Its 1:20 pm now, and a cab just parked outside my gate. I could hear the horn, and felt a rush in my blood. Wow ! I'm just about to meet this girl after a decade almost. How did she look now, was my first thought. I hurried myself, picked my necessary items, locked my door and rushed out to the gate. And there she was, in a pale yellow dress that complemented her wheatish skin and she was looking gorgeous. The driver opened the door for me, and as I sat in, she tight hugged me. I felt the same warmth and comfort with her energy, just as the olden days. Some feelings never change. Not in all cases though. I looked at her and asked, "So, what's the plan? Where do you intend to take me? By the way, Avantika, you haven't change much, dear. You look fabulous as always with that radiant smile I love so much ".

"You didn't change either ", she said. "lets look for a cozy place, where there won't be much rush. But, they should serve good food, haa ! I really want to make the most out of the time we spend together. "

So we decided to look into this very elegant Bistro, a little away from the city hustle- bustle. It looked a decent place with greenery all around. The ambience was delightful, could feel a homely touch, and they served exotic food. I too visited this place for the first time and got carried away. We chose a corner table, out in the open space that looks a sort of patio, and made ourselves comfortable. We started with fresh organic juices and starters, and gradually went through each course. Here I would like to mention, that, My motto is not to share about the food or an outing with a close friend, but to point out a serious note, to you all. A plight that our society deals with, at a huge number on regular basis, yet it's a hushed up matter from time immemorial. Coming back to the meeting, our discussions too gradually proceeded towards this matter, to which I will come eventually.

After our first course, I asked her, "So how's life ? What are you doing these days?, did you get into anything for yourself ?, career wise I mean ".

I know she has two kids to look after and is definitely a busy mom. But, as I had sensed that she wants to share something, I put out the question to her. Although she said, "All good ! life is as usual running on its own track "... yet, I could sense the pain in her voice, and as I looked at her, I noticed that her eyes were moist.

"You can share with me anything, my dear, if that makes you feel lighter, I will be happy to help ", I told her. She immediately put her hand across the table and squeezed my palm and said, "I know, and that's the reason why I decided to meet you ".

Yet, I thought, she might be feeling uneasy and probably might not be ready to discuss as of now, and so I said, "Take your time Avantika ".

"Time is all I have taken, enough time, but now I am composed and I need to share my thoughts, in order to find peace within me ", came her prompt reply. So I said, "Ok ! Let's begin."

She choked a bit, as she started and her eyes became misty.

"It was around my late 30's, almost entering my 40th," she began....

"By then, I was free of my duties as a mother. I had an empty nest now, both the girls preferred to study elsewhere and so they had shifted to their respective Hostels. At first, it was going good and I felt relaxed, as I was free of workloads. Arranging special breakfast, lunch and dinner items had to be minutely monitored, as everything from taste to quantity, had to be perfect, after all it was my duty to please everyone and see a smiling and content face always, is what I thought. Making everyone happy was my priority always, although it was tiring at times, specially when helpers took their weekend off. But I somehow managed. "

"It was a busy schedule for me ", she continued. "I would start early at 5am and continue till 11:30 pm till I hit the bed. Although mechanically, I was somewhat a happy soul, at least I thought so. I sometimes managed a few outings with friends and extended families. With friends, it would be somewhat lively but it was a rare incident. My outings were more of family gathering, boring mostly and not to mention the gossiping now and then."

She paused and smiled, "most of the time it would be the same people, same traditional food with variable changes here and there. I would always be excited before the programs but returned home at times unhappy and probably this left me unsatisfied. I actually am the black sheep of the family. So, whenever there was a family gathering, my cousins, their children, my siblings, stole the show. Being a very close knit family, they were all supportive too, asking for each other's wellbeing, health issues and other problems but gossiping about others in general was a highlighted agenda. I always had been an observer. Although it did not matter much for anyone, as I was not an important personality for them. My husband would always get his due respect, I must say. He has this superb quality of making anyone in the room burst out into laughter, at his comic wit. He is a wag no doubt, but would himself never even smile while conversing. It is a quality indeed, but we at home were always bored. This period of my life was also for a short span, because we kept moving around for these postings, as you know ". she said.

I could understand her travail, as working for an organization where transfer is inevitable within every two to three years, it could not be enjoyable for sure .

"This time, after a period of 12 years, it was only me and my husband moving together to a new township ", she shared. "The children were not with us for the first time. They were happily studying at their choice of institutes and were enjoying their newly found freedom. Here we were, entering a new phase of life where I was introduced to myself as a loner, with no change in my husband's routine. I didn't know how to cope with my free time. Initially, for a few days I got busy with the house arrangements, but then what, life turned monotonous. My husband would be on duty by 9:30 in the morning and would return home around 8:30 pm. Workaholic by nature, he always brought his office home. These days computer also helps in this regard. It became difficult for me, how long can one paint and sketch, read books, watch television?. New place, new environment and not many known people to interact with, I hardly had any circle at all. This resulted in loneliness and then heralded to the first taste of depression," She sighed.

I could feel the hollowness but was short of words, what do I say is what I wondered.

"I did not realize it at first," she kept continuing. "One afternoon after lunch, I took to rest for a while. Within few minutes, my whole body was twisting up on its own and beyond my control. It was not exactly pain that I felt, it was rather a sensation unexplainable. I felt it all over my body. The twists at first felt ok, but within seconds, I sensed that my nerves would wreck up totally as I could not put a stop to the movement. I thought it would be over soon, yet within half an hour, it brought tears in my eyes. I complained to my husband, but there was no response. He was as usual busy with his office work. It was Sunday, and by evening, I had started crying out loud. My own behavior was shocking to me. I generally have a lot of patience, but this time I could not manage from reacting. I decided to move outside on my own, and look for a doctor. I changed my dress and was at the main door, when my husband noticed my behavior and got a clear message that I was upset. Its then that he came after me and enquired, 'where are you going? You don't even know anybody out here '

I gave a blank look at him and snapped, " I need a doctor. Its been more than 4 hours now, that I am in pain and after repeated complaints, you hardly bothered. "

" I don't know any doctor yet, we have just settled in this city, remember? " , came his reply.

"Well, its all about going out hunting medical help, who needs to know a doctor?," I asked, "anyways, I am going in search for one. "

Avantika's expression, right then, showed her pain and resentment. She looked at me and said,

"He followed me quietly after that. We reached the corner of the street, when he called up a colleague and enquired. This guy, decided to help immediately and within 15 minutes, he was at our destination to pick us up. We hopped into his car and reached a doctor's chamber. It was quite late by then considering the city's condition. Although my cramps had subsided a little, I still felt weak. There were a few patients before me and so we had to wait. When my turn came, the doctor simply listened to my problems and later asked me a few personal questions, such as.... my day to day activities, family time, joyful outings, how many children I have, how much time I spend with them, and so on.

After that, the doctor asked me to wait outside and send my husband in. I could hear their conversation. The doctor informed my husband that I am going through the syndrome of mild depression and I needed help. Since it was only the initial stage, things could improve. I should be given time, taken out for short trips, some fun time together with family now and then..... is what he suggested. He also said that, staying within the four walls always, will take me for a ride through memory lanes which could result to further deterioration. To this, my husband very coolly responded that he didn't have time. So the doctor said, "Well, its my duty to advise what is best for my patient. To follow it or not is your choice ".

This moment Avantika almost broke down. I couldn't understand how to console her, because this is not what I would myself tolerate. I passed her a glass of water and asked her to calm down. By then we had finished lunch. I ordered two fresh- lime soda, as I wanted her to relax. She then carried on again ...

" The doctor suggested some medicines and we were back on our way home. Next day by mid-afternoon, my medications came home. I goggled the names and found them to be anti- depressant. I was a little reluctant to take those medicines because I didn't feel that it was depression totally. I kept convincing myself that.... 'of course being alone and away from the children for the first time, gives pain. But then, it happens with every family, as kids will move out now or later,'.... I thought out loud.

So, after a month, I stopped taking the medicine. My husband then suggested that I should visit my kids for a few days. This was an exciting idea for me and so by the next weekend, I joined them. Few days were exciting, but for how long? I had to be back home again." she said.

I looked at the watch, it was almost 4pm. We were still sitting there after lunch. So I invited her home. Somehow, I managed to convince her to spend the night with me. We drove back home with a stop here and there for important grocery items. When we reached home, I made some good coffee for us, and with homemade muffins, we had a jolly time together. She later helped me prepare a light dinner. We shared our memories of past days, that we had spent together. It was an awesome moment, to recollect so many fond memories and be joyful. It was dinner time soon and I was surprised how time can run fast when we are in best company. After dinner, we shared the room that night. I wanted her to pour out all her emotions that she had stored within herself, for quite long now.

"Avantika how was your journey back home, and what happened after you got back. Was your health better by then? ", - I asked.

"After meeting my children and spending gala time with them, I felt rejuvenated for a while. But the boredom that followed within three four months took a toll on my health," She said. " I soon suffered from nervous breakdown and had to be rushed to the hospital again. Although the crisis was met, I knew this was it, that this was only the beginning".

"What did the doctors suggest ? ", I asked

"This time too, they had the same suggestion ", she sighed , " Luckily, my husband too suffered issues at his workplace this time, and urged for transfer on the pretext of my physical problem. He managed to get posted to a different city within the next two months. But this time too, fate played a new game with me. "

I looked at her surprisingly, "What was the problem this time ? ", I enquired.

"This time, he was posted to a hill station up North. Words will fall short to describe its beauty. People, all I knew, went gaga about it, but my doctors simply said, 'No'.

"And why is it so ? ", I questioned

"It was my physical status. The phase of depression that they had earlier diagnosed, took a different turn now with changes in symptoms of my ailment that kept continuing, and eventually it resulted to neurological disorder. Structural abnormalities in the spinal cord and other nerves, resulted to muscle weakness, poor coordination, loss of sensation in some areas, and pain all over the body. So, in such cases, ... dampness, moisture in environment, chilly wintry weather, can aggravate my condition further. As such, it was a strict no from the medical team. So I had to shift to our home in Chennai , all by myself for more than a year. My husband would visit at times, but I had to manage all alone "she said

"O no ! But its curable, right ? ", I asked

"No dear, of date, its only manageable ", prompt came her response.

I wondered why. How can someone deal with such experiences throughout his / her life. "So what is the solution to this? ", I enquired again.

"So far, the only solution is, lifestyle changes, physiotherapy, pain management, medications and specific diet, and that's it ". She answered.

It broke me down to the core, for, I noticed several times, that she was whimpering while she spoke. I was speechless and although I could anticipate her agony, it was still difficult to measure her pain. I hesitated to sympathize, because she didn't need it. She was battling pain all by herself and very bravely. I applauded her instead.

" You are amazing Avantika ! How do you even manage it ? I truly can't feel how bad the pain is, but I do understand that, it is not an easy task to deal with mood swings and body aches simultaneously. Hats off to you my dear. But tell me one thing, how frequently do you face the attacks ? " I questioned.

"Its always there, 24×7, darling," she smiled as she informed.

I looked at her amused, astonished and doleful, all at the same time. I hold her hand and just remained silent for some time as I could not voice out anything. I could not hold my emotion in control and I looked away. She turned me towards her and said very calmly, "Come on ! It's a part and parcel of life. It does not bother me at all, not anymore. Yes, its difficult at times to move around, but what can I do about it ?, crying will not help for sure, is all I know ".

"How did you grow to be so matured and when ?" I talked to myself but aloud. For I remember her, as this bubbly girl next door. Always joyous and full of life. Why does she have to go through this suffering?

She was looking away. Although misty eyed, yet she managed to hold herself strong.

"You know what, I too broke down totally, at first. I couldn't bear the pain. My entire body felt so alien. I spent innumerable sleepless nights and mostly kept awake crying. I couldn't take it, that all along I had been on my toes and you know it well, and suddenly I was unable to move around in freedom. I was always there for everyone, regularly calling up family members, enquiring about friends, ready to help neighbors at odd hours. And suddenly here I was, helplessly in bed, for months at a stretch. I could not walk properly. The pain was so intense, that my body would swell up, causing fever. At times, I had to take 5/6 aspirin a day .I did fight a battle with my body Anna and I never complained. But what I could not take easily was, silence from all those people whom I considered to be my family and friends. A few friends did keep touch, but for a while. Strangely, not a single relative called up those days to enquire my whereabouts. I had to take break from my routine calls and chats, as I could not hold the mobile even for five minutes. Since I was the initiator always, calls from my end were nil at this time. Surprisingly, my silence too didn't bother anyone" She paused for a while.

I silently passed towards her , a glass of water. She took a sip or two, and continued to speak.

"I was really surprised, " she said .

"Probably these thoughts kept disturbing me so much, every single day, that it triggered my depressive mind. I started feeling helpless. I was all by myself and depended on my household helps. They were solely the ones who were around me, and on whom I had to depend at the time of crisis. You know what ! bad time teaches us several lessons of life, and I have learnt mine. So, initially what troubled me, became my strength with passing days. I no longer cry because I understood that, I have to stabilize myself for the sake of my children, till they would remain dependent on me. I convinced myself that, there will be a time sooner or later, when I would no longer be a necessity, even in their life, and

I was okay with the thought. I don't put a blame on anyone, as we all are on our own - own journey. "

I listened to her quietly. There was no longer any sign of helplessness in her voice now, and neither in her expression. She was calm, and I simply kept watching her in admiration.

"I have decided", she continued, "to do my bit of responsibility, as profoundly possible, for everyone who seek my help. But, the day I start feeling totally dejected, I will simply walk out on every relation, and lead my life on my own, embracing the pain and agony, and will explore the unknown terrain with utmost pride on myself "

She sounded very confident and determined, at this time, and I simply felt proud of her self-worth. No matter what, this lady deserves respect on all terms. I nodded my head in her support, and trust me, this was all that she needed. She was already victorious on her own. I cannot help but keep admiring her for the way she conducted herself. I didn't see her vulnerable side, but, she surely tackled and did overcome her Cimmerian isolation in a very splendid way indeed. I only assured her that I would always be by her side without fail. And slowly, as we turned around to pass away into sleep, I quietly saluted her renewed vigor. All she needed was my patient ears for her pain, not the physical problem but the emotional troubles. I wonder, why people in today's time, cannot be a little compassionate towards their someone own.

I greeted her in the morning, around 8:50 am, with a cup of ginger flavored black tea, just as the way she preferred. She sat up with a jerk as she looked at the clock, and then passed a smile and said,

"Hi ! Good morning, I did sleep peacefully after a long time".

We chatted over tea, some girlie gossips, and then I got busy with breakfast preparations. We had a long breakfast session at the table, just having good time together. As we finished, she expressed her desire to leave within an hour, as she had an appointment with her doctor. We promised to keep a regular touch, and visit each other once, every year. Or at least, plan vacations together. The very thought boosted up my energy and I felt rejuvenated. My boring days saw some color and excitement. She was ready by her time, and I walked her up till her vehicle. As she departed, she turned around once , with a smile of serenity and satisfaction, and my heart bloomed with extra love.

What did I do ?, I questioned myself, it was only a whole day of my peaceful ears for her situation and my silent admiration for her. But then, that was all she needed and desired. With a sigh- I got back to my daily chores.

Two

When Avantika left, I kept to myself for sometime. Each passing day, I thought over the situation that she was in, and it kept me occupied mentally, trying to understand the reasoning behind each perception and it disturbed me a lot. Eventually, I kept thinking about all my loved ones and their wellbeing.

One evening, as I sat with a cup of coffee, all by myself, I looked into my laptop and scrolled down old time pictures that I had saved as memories of near and dear ones. As I did so, I came over the pictures of a very close family friend. I know them from a long time and so closely that, we almost seemed to belong from the same family. But unfortunately, due to each of our busy schedule, we lost touch with passing time, so much so that, we hardly gathered up ourselves to enquire about each other's health and wellbeing.

Although, it's a necessity to keep constant connection and enquire the whereabouts of people close to us , we do fail.

The very thought made me nostalgic and I immediately picked up my phone and called up their place. They are sweet and lovely people, very gentle by nature. The lady of the house, is a good old friend and very dear to me. Her husband, a much loved personality in the neighborhood, is a jolly man and very helpful and supportive by nature. He is a gentleman thoroughly. Their only daughter, a cute little girl, used to spend a lot of her time at our apartment when we were sharing the same building in a different locality. The memories brought a pleasant fondness of her, right at this moment. When I moved to this place, we still frequented at each other's quite often. But as the pandemic approached, in fact even before that, we could not visit, and neither have we interacted much. Its been more than three-four years now. How time flies, is what I kept pondering on.

After the second try to reach them over phone , Manjusha's voice came , sweet as usual, on the other side.

"Hi Dear!, how are you all doing ?," I asked. "Sorry haa ! I couldn't be in touch with you all since quite long now. Hopefully you all are doing good in this trying time ".

She said that all was good, yet her voice sounded shaky. I was not convinced, as, this is not how Manjusha usually is. Though she is very sober, yet something was amiss in her tone today. So I said, "Manjusha, you know very well that you can always count on me. Why is it, that I feel, all are not okay, that you are not in right mood ? Is everything fine with Bhatt Saab ? And what about Rucha? missing the girl a lot ".

"Rucha is our concern Anna, ", her voice cracked up .

I felt a jolt immediately. What could be wrong with this charming little girl ? With a guilt conscious, that I didn't try to be on track often, I asked her, "Why? What's the matter with her? "

"Rucha is finding problem coping up with life on all aspects, although we tried to support her, it is still difficult. We are in a critical situation ."Manjusha said.

Now, that was a shocking news for me. I never expected this. So I said, "Listen Manjusha, although it's the pandemic and movement or visiting people are restricted, yet I would like to come up to your place within an hour, if you would allow me".

"O yeah ! Sure," she replied. "We would be delighted to have you around. Please do come over. We shall be looking forward to your presence anytime soon ".

I was so relaxed within myself immediately. At least, within a while, I will be there to share their problem. And Rucha of all, she's my darling. Oh no ! Why do children need to suffer ?" is all I questioned God. I started pacing up and down the room. No ! I can't waste anymore time, I thought to myself. I walked up to the washroom, freshened up, and changed my dress. I picked up my car keys and immediately drove out.

All along the way, I was only wondering, what could go so wrong with the girl. She is barely fourteen years now. I was anxious to find out the cause and couldn't relax as I drove up to their home. Within fifty minutes, I was there, as traffic was thin. I parked my car, and noticed that the dogs had started growling. As I approached the main door, I could hear footsteps behind the closed door. I reached for the bell, and just then Manjusha opened the door and stood there ushering me in. Just as I stepped in, she looked at me and broke down into tears. I hugged her tight, instantly. Bhatt Saab, her husband, followed in and we all sat there in the lobby. There was no sign of Rucha. Her father informed that she was with one of her friend from the neighbours, in her room.

" What do I say Manjusha , except sorry , for taking so long time to reach out " . I broke the silence . " I really got tied up with the natty – gritty and then , this pandemic happened .What is it that is troubling Rucha ? And why couldn't you inform me ? "

I looked at her and she was teary eyed.

"You need not apologize dear, I can totally understand," She replied. "Yes, I should have called, but I hope you can gather what we are going through ".

She looked at her husband, and then looked at me and very softly said, "Rucha was all ok, Anna. Very jolly and bubbly was my child. She was doing great in her academics, there were no interference or pressure from our side. She had her own way always and her teachers were also happy with her performance. Suddenly, out of nowhere, she had started avoiding our calls, could not attend her classes regularly and often fell sick. A friend of hers, informed us that Rucha spent sleepless nights and then would fall asleep during her classes. I was shocked, as she never shared these with me, whenever we communicated. So, I enquired the matter with her. At first she denied, but could not keep away her emotions for long, and confessed the matter to be true. She keeps crying whenever we try to talk to her. Since then, we are disturbed, as we do not know what to do. I tried talking out her problems, but she keeps saying that, as such, there is no reason, yet, she cannot sleep peacefully throughout the night."

"Why don't you seek medical help for her ?", I asked. "Its not a big deal Manjusha. These days most people suffer from this condition. And so, people are open to psychological problems. And our concern should be our daughter's health. This sort of issue, if addressed early, can be cured faster than you imagine. What do you think, Bhatt Saab ? ", I asked addressing her husband.

He was tensed, as I could anticipate from his facial expression, yet he tried to smile softly.

"Yes, you are right Anna, we should go for it. This is what we were discussing, as a few close friends too, suggested the same." He then looked at Manjusha and back at me and said, "Can you accompany us ? I mean, if possible of course. I too will come, but I would prefer to wait outside, as you take them in, through the session."

"Why not ! ", I said, "but don't you think Rucha would love to have both her parents by her side ?"

"Yes, definitely, but she wouldn't be uncomfortable if you accompany her, knowing the bond she shares with you. Maybe it will help her open up more with the doctor. ", he suggested.

I didn't wish to waste any further time in considering the matter, as my sole intention was to get Rucha medical help immediately. So, without hesitation, I agreed instantly, and we decided to book an appointment with a psychiatrist, the very next morning. Her father had booked the appointment for 11:30 am next day. After a little more discussion with them, I met Rucha in her room. It was almost after three-four years. She was out of the city for her studies, and so there was little I could do .

The girl looked pale, her eyes were set back from sleep deprived. She was happy to see me and we spent some time together, yet I failed to see that enthusiasm she always had. Her mother informed that she is much better now, and I too believe so, because home environment is always better to cheer up the mood of children her age, as, parents do their best to keep the children happy. I left their home around 9:00pm, with a hope that together we could bring happiness into their circumstances.

I could not easily fall asleep that night. A set of tired eyes, a disturbed mind and a worried face, kept me awake till late night. I woke up around 5:30am, took my bath and sat for meditation. I had to cool my mind and appear fresh before Rucha. I need to encourage and motivate her, to an extent that she would forget her problems. I still did not know what could be the reason for her sadness. I was only looking forward to the right time, when everything would be fine with her.

Around 9:30 am, I called them up and informed that, within twenty minutes, I would reach their home and pick them up. I drove to their place and after collecting them, we headed towards the Clinic. Her father too accompanied us and this cheered me up. It is necessary at this moment, that she gets true support from both her parents. When we reached there, her father decided to wait outside, until he was physically needed by the doctor. Within a while, Rucha's turn came and we entered the cabin. The doctor gestured us to sit down, and then gently enquired her problem. Manjusha shared her bit, and then the doctor asked if we could allow Rucha to have solo conversation with him.

Both Manjusha and me agreed, and we stepped out to join her father. We sat there impatiently, as Rucha continued for some time more in the doctor's company. Around ten minutes later, Rucha came out and informed that the doctor wished to see us. We all went back and sat with him. He even arranged an extra chair for us. He then asked a few more questions on certain points. Within a short span, I noticed that Manjusha was looking upset as the doctor was hardly listening to her. He rather preferred talking to her husband, and simply kept his point of views, regarding the matter.

Bhatt Saab, being an extremely polite person could do nothing much and simply kept nodding to everything that the doctor suggested. But I could sense that Manjusha was feeling frustrated. The doctor suggested some medicines and asked them to report after two weeks. We all walked out silently and as we sat in the car, Manjusha broke her silence-.

"Isn't it a bit rude on the doctor's part to ignore on what I had to say ? ", she vented. "Being her mother, and a constant companion for so many years, won't I be knowing her condition a bit better? The doctor should have had more patience and be amenable towards our opinion too, before being impulsive and suggesting medicines. " She snapped.

I understood, that this session did not help them at all and so, I suggested them for a second opinion I took them straight to another hospital nearby and we asked for an appointment with the head of the department. After half an hour's wait, Rucha's turn came. This time I suggested that both parents should accompany her, while I wait outside. It was a twenty minute session this time, and they came out satisfied, at least not tensed.

I looked at Manjusha and she smiled. "The doctor said, its nothing much to worry about. Its an anxiety and crisis period that she is tackling now. Most children do, and probably, home sickness also played a major role ", she reported.

"So any medication suggested for her ? ", I asked .

"No ", came her father's response. "She simply suggested that Rucha must take sufficient rest, as stress level is quite high. Also, we must communicate with her from a more approachable space. She needs to interact more and that will help her share her problems with an open mind. "

Being a therapeutic counselor, I decided to be of help to her. Although she should be seeing her doctor whenever needed, is what we decided. I dropped them home and on my way, ordered a pizza for lunch. Although I did nothing, yet I felt extremely exhausted. I thought for a while, how tiring it must be for all who undergo stress related issues. I reached home, and by then the delivery boy was also at my doorstep with the pizza package. While I savored my lunch, I decided to share her case with a doctor friend of mine.

In the evening, I felt a little relaxed and thought it would be the best time to call up this friend and discuss the problem. As I related to him about her issue, he silently listened and then dazed me with a shocking news.

He said, "Do you know what !, this pandemic had given rise to depressions like never before. Yes, it was always there, but lockdowns exhibited job losses and also losses to business and many other financial, domestic and emotional set back. It had affected people on various aspects, which resulted to extreme level of such cases. I have a personal experience of losing a fellow doctor's daughter recently "

I didn't know what to say. I can understand common people suffering, but a doctor family in such condition was beyond my imagination.

"What had happened to her ?" I asked.

To which he replied, "it was early this month, that a colleague informed me about this doctor losing his younger daughter, a doctor we know very closely. It was shocking news for me. And what is more surprising for the fraternity is, both the parents are doctors, yet they couldn't manage to save their child from taking her life in a dreaded way ".

It shook me from within, totally. What is happening with humanity?, Why can't they give a fight to their unstable mind?; I know its easier said than done. But its not impossible, if we are ready to try. People will question my strength in such a situation, and for sure. Well, let me then come up with my share of a sting from this bitter-sweet bug.

Three

I too almost fell a victim to the grip of these unwelcoming phenomena. Its only my inner strength and will power that kept me going, and prevented all the illusions to clouden over my mind.

It was about seven - eight years back. my only child, had just left home for further studies. It was the first time that I ever stayed away from my child. Although difficult, first two years passed off simply well, as we kept meeting during the vacations. Then came the real challenge when it was time for moving further away from home, that too abroad. Although I knew deep within, that, this time it would be a totally far away scenario, and it would not at all be possible to reach out each other, yet it had become impossible to accept the reality. I soon started brooding over my empty nest syndrome. Suddenly, I could not fathom how to manage my spare time. This resulted to mild depression initially, and then, I unfortunately had to undergo the traumatic suffering of this gruesome disease and cruel consequences of '*Herpes Zoster*'

Immediately after the attack of this unwanted malady, I had consulted doctors who unfortunately treated me the wrong way, as they identified the pain with kidney stone problem. They kept administering me medicine according to what they diagnosed. Two doctors having done the same mistake, is still an unbelievable irony. Both of them carry forwarded the treatment on the same line. Within two weeks, I realized that something was going tremendously wrong. I changed the doctor again. Third time now, I could by then, feel some rashes taking bad turn on my lower body parts and my back as well as the torso area.

So, the lady doctor whom I was consulting this time, I deliberately made her see the rashes, and she exclaimed at the sight of the horrible harrowing disease that I was undergoing. Although the treatment became easier, as it was crystal clear now, yet damage had already been done to my body by then. I suffered a setback for a prolonged period. This condition left me bed ridden for about six months. Out of which two months went extremely bad .It was a terrible experience one can ever think of, and the grilling effect of pre and post herpes is horrendous. I have faint memory of two months in particular, as I had almost lost my senses at that time. Doctors kept asking me to be in constant company of loved ones. They wanted me to be happy and cheerful so that I become capable to show courage in the face of adversity.

To my dismay, no one ever asked me if I was doing okay, let alone my expectation of help from anyone. At this crucial time I was expecting that someone dear to me, from my family, would be with me even if it was only a virtual togetherness. But no one even thought to ask why I had not been calling them. My helper then, came to my rescue. She was the only person who kept asking me how I was doing, gave me company for an hour daily and brought food for me from her end. I could not walk properly for almost a year. I kept asking myself, "why do I deserve this loneliness? when I always had been there for everyone who sought my help ". The doctors in my immediate family, never bothered to enquire how I was coping with my situation. During this time, I realized, everything in life is a farce.

We stick to several relations in life, considering them to be our only existence. In reality, no one actually matters.

Four

My own problematic period is a turning point for me. I started visualizing life in general, from a different perspective now. Initially there were a lot of purging moments, which I had gradually succeeded to shed off, and it became easier to let go of situations and emotions that tormented me from within. I built, somewhere into the core of my being, a great strength to combat my emotions and suffering, emotions that were useless. These emotions come from expectations, from family and other sources, that hardly benefit us and as a result we manifest meaningless pain. And the sooner we realize it, the better.

In my case, I understood that these emotions were only holding me back from my true happiness and instigating me rather, to be harsh with myself, thus blocking all positive outcome that I wish to adorn in my life.

It is no doubt difficult to come into terms with these feelings. But trust me, it's not impossible. We as Homo sapiens, are blinded by our own foggy mind, and feel enslaved by our own foreshortened thoughts. It is us who allow others to take control of our composure. We easily trust people when they assure us to be by our side in our need, but when we do approach for help, their dramatic denial comes to us as a surprise. We find it difficult then, to accept the reality and we start blaming circumstances and people, connected to our situation. We prefer self-sabotaging rather than accepting that it is only and only our duty to take responsibility of our own life. Reality is, everyone have their own way of dealing with life, and they can rightfully exercise their behavior towards us, in the manner that pleases them most.

So far, whatever incidents I had shared, I pondered on every situation, including my personal experiences and I came towards solutions that helped me and also my earlier mentioned friends. Hence, I wish to take help of this project, to express my knowledge on matters that can help someone to overcome their inner turmoil's with simple measures and also help others in similar situations. All we must understand is that, life is not a bed of all roses for everyone. Few people are fortunate to experience such a luxury. In the present scenario of the pandemic affecting society, depression is a very common issue these days. It always had been so, but this issue was preferred to be brushed away under the carpet, instead of addressing it.

Earlier, it was manageable to deal with the problems silently. People were so busy that they hardly bothered to enquire about friends, family, and neighbors. Hence, it had been easy to keep such matters behind closed doors. Although it is not a matter of shame, yet it was always considered a hindrance to people's pride. Nobody ever wanted to share the vulnerability of someone in the family going through the issue and how they suffered. Everyone feared that family prestige would be hampered, a thought which obviously came from their ego. It was always looked upon as ... "what would people say, if they come to know ? "

Why should we allow others to be judgmental towards us and bother about opinions that should not matter at all. Who cares what others have got to say, when none of those people would even come forward to help. Why bother about such filth that comes from sources that hardly matter. People in your life, who are only for entertainment, will anyway judge. Those who care will stand by your side.

Depression is an important issue that should be dealt with, just as any other disease, because it reflects our state of mind. Our mental health is important, for it regulates us towards a healthy body. You may not be wealthy by possession of riches but if you have a peace of mind and a sound body, you are the most resourceful being and the happiest soul for that matter. Learn to accept reality and go with the flow. It is in your own hand to create a better life for yourselves, as nothing is ever written on stepping stones. I want to say this to each and everyone, ... It is possible to dream and bring those into fruition, only when you are ready to work with your inner knowing. We must all take the reigns of our life in our own hands because we are our best judge.

You can approach others for suggestions, and you will get a handful of it, but then, ask yourselves if those advises truly contribute in your life. You will be amazed that majority time ,those suggestions do not work for you at all. Even if it does, you are to take actions to see the best result. No one does that for you.

So, try not to indulge yourself into people pleasing, rather work on yourself to attain your highest potential. Your success will bring all those people closer to you, who had been ignoring your presence so far. No matter in what situation you find yourselves, always trust that there is some force which will provide you support that you need, in every possible way.

So, my dear friends never give up hope and lose yourself to the illusion of darkness. There is always a ray of light at the end of your hard days. Both night and day are inevitable and we cannot change its course. Can we ever deny the existence of the Sun and the Moon? How can we, and why should we even try? They both play equal role in the pattern or process we understand as day and night. They are both equally important for the Universal truth of life and its existence. It is the same with us. Our Ego and Authenticity goes together to enhance our life with enjoyment and realization. We must embrace both and keep working on our own shadows to bring out the better us from within. One must understand that, life throws challenges towards us, so that we get to learn some beautiful lesson. Experiences of hardship and joy comes hand in hand, but, as we concentrate on our difficulties alone, we suffer emotional setbacks. Ask yourselves, do you brood on your joyful moments and question its existence? Do you keep asking "Oh why did these joyous moments occur in our life? "

If not, why keep lamenting on your painful experiences. Accept them as lessons of life and walk ahead, leaving the past memories behind. Help yourself to lighten up your baggage as you move forward in your life's journey instead of making it heavy and difficult. These extra baggage's of the past will not serve any purpose in your life further. Condition your thoughts to believe that all those who enter your life at several stages, and gives you pain in the going, were meant to do so, because they serve the role of teachers in your life. Take the lessons, be thankful to them and then walk ahead on your journey to open yourselves into happier times. Once you understand the whole episode in a manner I had just mentioned, you will find it easier to release the situation and everyone connected to your circumstances

into light and love, and you will find yourself capable to carry
only fond memories ahead with you.

Penult

At this point, I wish to share my opinion on how to combat your situations and come out of the agony that acts as a dampener in your life. I wish to reach out to all those innocent hearts that at some point enters this journey of dolefulness, not by choice but mostly because are unenlightened.

Whatever you may have faced, or maybe you are still going through, gives pain a lot. You might need to let go of things, relations, work places and even homes where you feel the closest. You are so attached to the comfort and adjustments they bring, that the very thought of leaving them behind gives you pain. Yes, change is painful, but the growth on the other hand that awaits to be your pleasant future is alluring at the same time. Understand that nothing is as painful as staying stuck-up somewhere you don't belong at all. Even if that decision of moving ahead gives you pain, yet take action on the decision, and you will find yourself in a much more blessed situation than you can even imagine. Trust in surrendering, because your faith can move the mountains that stand as your barrier. Never let your fear or lack and loss decide your future. Its only when you start taking the risks that you are pushed towards, you will find yourself confident and fearless at a certain point of time, and that's when you suddenly achieve success, because your confidence makes you independent and strong.

Start believing that the struggles which are only temporary, comes along your way only to shape you as a better YOU, for your own good and for your purpose ahead. If you do surrender, to an unseen source, much mightier than you and your thoughts, you will definitely be guided to the right path, the path that you have to walk your walk. It might be confusing and challenging at times, and you will feel urged to give up. But standing tall and taking the steps anyway will lead you towards the right direction, helping you to achieve all that you have aspired for. Do understand, all that you ask for, may not always appear to you in the manner that you have visualized, but it definitely will turn out to be way better than you expected. At times, we all have to go through our worst to get the best that we deserve.

Nature has proved similar situations to us in so many ways, but we remain ignorant of the messages. The seeds that we plant do grow into fruit bearing trees but they also go through several hardships of facing harshness of survival they come across in the process of growing. So, can't we too learn to embrace the storms in our life ?. If you learn the art of calming down yourselves, the storm will pass with ease. Only patience leads us to the door of happiness. No matter how worse the time is, that you are facing at your bereaved moment, do not be pushed around by your fearful thoughts.

Rather allow the dreams in your heart to lead you ahead and someday soon, you will be in a space you are most comfortable. Always make healthy choices and you will never fail to be happy. Life might not give you all that you desire, but with time you will get all that you deserve, only carry your loads with grace and comfort, and allow to get lightened from time to time in the most perfect manner that suits you. Right things will surely appear in your life unexpectedly, trust is what is needed because everything will happen at the perfect time and one day everything will make sense. We need to choose hope over doubts and anything we want, we can make it possible. The ones whom we see as successful people, have had their own share of struggle. Either we choose to fight and shine or we accept the ordinary and live an unsatisfied life.

Nobody can promise you your success and smile, it is you and only you who can decorate your life with all meaningful bounties that you gather in every step of your journey. Its our mind that gives us an experience of fearful thoughts, whereas in reality you might find how easy it is to conquer over fear if you can strongly intend to. It is our own inner strength that allows us to achieve our goals only by deciding to walk away from what hurts us most . Believe that you are powerful all by yourself to fight your hardships by never giving up. Its your struggle that develops your strength, not a happy and fun filled life always. You can successfully make yourself the personality you wish to become only if you believe in yourself.

My dear friends, my readers, if you find yourself in similar situations, please do not stop trying even if you are facing failure at present. Your efforts and hardship will lead you to your success at your right time. Keep your thoughts positive, be brave be strong and fight the challenges that peeks at your door and you will surprisingly win the battle because its only your determination and sacrifices that can set you free. A strong mind can make any and every situation turn into an opportunity. Be courageous and face every challenge in life, be strong be kind and support every other person in need of your help . Be generous , be grateful and nothing can stop you from achieving your goals in life.

Lag

To all my readers who are fortunate to have a blessed life, it's my earnest request, please do reach out with a smile on your face and a heart full of love and care, reach out to that every single person who needs your help. It is the universal law that when you think good for others, good things come as blessings in your life.

In the recent past, humanity started losing the essence of happiness, joy, peace and bliss in life and its only because each one of us tend to choose a life centered around our own needs, comfort and likings. We have lost our ability to think and act with our heart. The concept of love has lost its meaning altogether. Relationships are going bitter and to rocks as there are no true feelings and emotions attached. Why can't we wish good for others ? If we treat others with respect, the same will come back to us. Nobody else's success can limit us from gaining ours, yet we humans tend to pull down others emotionally or harm them by other means. Often people say, "good that this person is going through the particular pain. He / she deserves it ".

I wonder, why to rejoice in someone's pain even if they are not good at times? We can always be good in our thoughts and try to help them when they are in distress. Maybe our kind action and generosity will help those people to change their perspective and thus bring definite changes within them. You can always help someone with kind words and stop them from causing permanent damages just because they are temporarily upset. It is difficult for them to understand that at their moment of disparity, what mistakes they are about to make and so you can be their good thoughts, their positive attitude and guide them on the path of sanctity.

You can help them to heal by using your best assets and that is ... your heart full of love and an ear ready to listen to their agony and help them out. I would like to encourage each one of you to be that person, who stands by someone when they need God. Divinity exists within us and not somewhere in the Sky. You cannot expect to be rewarded for what you have achieved, but you will definitely be honored for what you have done to help others. We can at least try, to be that person who we would love to meet each day. Just as we wish to be praised for our capabilities, we also should point out the good in others. We need not prove anybody but we can feel the strength within ourselves, when we help others despite of struggling with our own personal demons.

Making everyone happy is neither in your hands and nor is it possible but to be the reason of someone's smile and to be a part of someone's happiness is the best you can do to make your life happy. By giving ease and comfort, happiness and joy to others, it can only make you richer each day. So, be the support possible for the people in need just at the right time , because, when you are good to others you are the best to yourself. You can touch so many hearts even without knowing and will become their fond memories even when you are gone, so let your own good actions remain as your legacy forever.

Mostly, people say .... "oh why should I bother what others are going through. I have my cup full of unhappy moments and nobody is asking me ". Well, start asking yourself if you are happy being cornered, or would you love to have someone who stands by you when you are feeling low. Why not be the one to bring the change in collective thoughts. It doesn't cost anyone anything to be that person who encourages others to look into their dreams with all hope and faith, to root someone when they are almost in tears.

Trying time knocks every other person's door, only we do not know what they all are going through. So please be kind, be compassionate and understanding. Make it a point to ask how they feel whenever you see someone gloomy because they do wait and wish for someone to enquire and care about their situation. Yes I know, many a times we ourselves go through such a rough situation that we can't even think of helping others. Yet, remember that you don't need to go through perfect circumstances to inspire others. Let others know how you deal with your imperfections and that will inspire them to handle their situations better.

No one actually needs your sympathy, neither is someone in distress, looking out to exploit and take advantage of others . Some do require empathy to get out of troublesome issues that are mostly mindful. Why not be the anchor someone needs so desperately. Its only if we each try to reach out to a few, we can change the condition of our society, which we all wish to see.

Come.... let us together try and help to bring little happiness in every home, and smile on every single face we look at, every single day. Let us convince ourselves and keep saying......

Yes!!! We can walk up to a person in pensive mood and say,

"Hey! You Are Never Alone.... I Stand By Your Side To Be The Moral Strength You Need Right Now. "

Let us all be the change we are looking for......

www.ingramcontent.com/pod-product-compliance
Lightning Source LLC
LaVergne TN
LVHW041756190726